Sea Otters

by Margo Gates

BLASTOFF! READERS

BELLWETHER MEDIA • MINNEAPOLIS, MN

Note to Librarians, Teachers, and Parents:

Blastoff! Readers are carefully developed by literacy experts and combine standards-based content with developmentally appropriate text.

Level 1 provides the most support through repetition of high-frequency words, light text, predictable sentence patterns, and strong visual support.

Level 2 offers early readers a bit more challenge through varied simple sentences, increased text load, and less repetition of high-frequency words.

Level 3 advances early-fluent readers toward fluency through increased text and concept load, less reliance on visuals, longer sentences, and more literary language.

Level 4 builds reading stamina by providing more text per page, increased use of punctuation, greater variation in sentence patterns, and increasingly challenging vocabulary.

Level 5 encourages children to move from "learning to read" to "reading to learn" by providing even more text, varied writing styles, and less familiar topics.

Whichever book is right for your reader, Blastoff! Readers are the perfect books to build confidence and encourage a love of reading that will last a lifetime!

This edition first published in 2014 by Bellwether Media, Inc.

No part of this publication may be reproduced in whole or in part without written permission of the publisher. For information regarding permission, write to Bellwether Media, Inc., Attention: Permissions Department, 5357 Penn Avenue South, Minneapolis, MN 55419.

Library of Congress Cataloging-in-Publication Data

Gates, Margo.
  Sea otters / by Margo Gates.
    p. cm. – (Blastoff! readers. Animal safari)
  Summary: "Developed by literacy experts for students in kindergarten through grade three, this book introduces sea otters to young readers through leveled text and related photos"– Provided by publisher.
  Audience: K to grade 3.
  Includes bibliographical references and index.
  ISBN 978-1-60014-915-3 (hardcover : alk. paper)
  1. Sea otter–Juvenile literature. I. Title. II. Series: Blastoff! readers. 1, Animal safari.
  QL737.C25G385 2014
  599.769515–dc23
                                                                        2013000889

Text copyright © 2014 by Bellwether Media, Inc. BLASTOFF! READERS and associated logos are trademarks and/or registered trademarks of Bellwether Media, Inc. SCHOLASTIC, CHILDREN'S PRESS, and associated logos are trademarks and/or registered trademarks of Scholastic Inc.

Printed in the United States of America, North Mankato, MN.

Contents

What Are Sea Otters?   4

Life in Water   6

Food   14

Pups   18

Glossary   22

To Learn More   23

Index   24

What Are Sea Otters?

Sea otters are **mammals** that live in the ocean. They stay near **coasts**.

Life in Water

Sea otters have thick fur. **Guard hairs** keep their skin warm and dry.

Webbed feet help sea otters move through water. Long, flat tails push them forward.

Sea otters float on their backs. They wrap their bodies in **seaweeds** so they do not **drift**.

They often rest in **rafts**. They hold on to one another to stay together.

Food

Hungry sea otters dive to the ocean floor. They search for snails, **shellfish**, and other food.

Then they float
as they eat. They
use rocks to break
open shellfish.

Pups

Sea otter **pups** are born in the water. They can float right away.

A mother holds her pup on her chest until it can swim. Otter hug!

Glossary

coasts—areas where the ocean meets land

drift—to move with the water to a different spot

guard hairs—long hairs on the outside of a sea otter's coat

mammals—warm-blooded animals that have backbones and feed their young milk

pups—baby sea otters

rafts—groups of sea otters that rest together

seaweeds—large weeds that grow in ocean water

shellfish—animals that live in water and have shells; clams and crabs are types of shellfish.

webbed feet—feet with thin skin that connects the toes

To Learn More

AT THE LIBRARY

Berger, Barbara. *A Lot of Otters*. New York, N.Y.: Philomel Books, 1997.

Tatham, Betty. *Baby Sea Otter*. New York, N.Y.: H. Holt and Co., 2005.

Waxman, Laura Hamilton. *Let's Look at Sea Otters*. Minneapolis, Minn.: Lerner Publications Company, 2011.

ON THE WEB

Learning more about sea otters is as easy as 1, 2, 3.

1. Go to www.factsurfer.com.

2. Enter "sea otters" into the search box.

3. Click the "Surf" button and you will see a list of related Web sites.

With factsurfer.com, finding more information is just a click away.

Index

bodies, 10
chest, 20
coasts, 4
dive, 14
drift, 10
float, 10, 16, 18
fur, 6
guard hairs, 6
mammals, 4
mother, 20
ocean, 4, 14
pups, 18, 20
rafts, 12
rest, 12
rocks, 16
seaweeds, 10

shellfish, 14, 16
skin, 6
snails, 14
tails, 8
water, 8, 18
webbed feet, 8
wrap, 10

The images in this book are reproduced through the courtesy of: Michael Gore/ Minden Pictures, front cover; Michael Gore/ FLPA, pp. 5, 9; Brian M. Guzzetti/ SuperStock, p. 7; Suzi Eszterhas/ Minden Pictures, p. 11; Milo Burcham/ Age Fotostock, p. 13; Minden Pictures/ SuperStock, p. 15; Greg Amptman's Undersea Discoveries, p. 15 (left & right); Lynsey Allan, p. 15 (middle); Matthias Breiter/ Minden Pictures, p. 17; Jurgen & Christine Sohns/ FLPA, p. 19; Milo Burcham/ SuperStock, p. 21.